SIMPLE THINGS
AND
SIMPLE THOUGHTS

by ELDON TAYLOR, Ph.D.

JAR Just Another Reality

Box 7116 Salt Lake City Utah 84107

Books by Dr. Eldon Taylor
available from
Just Another Reality Publishing:

Exclusively Fabricated Illusions

The Little Black Book

*Subliminal Communication:
Emperor's Clothes or Panacea?*

Subliminal Technology

Subliminal Learning

ISBN 0-916095-18-5

Dedication

DeMaupassant tells the story of a drone bee that, once trapped within his home, resisted efforts to be set free. The drone fought attempts aimed at directing him out the window where the meadow and wildflowers waited. Once out the window, the bee paused in midair as if to say, "Is this what that was all about!"

I believe that many of our "difficult" encounters are designed to set us free, but our resistance self-inflicts pain. In learning to let go and allow the natural flow of life, a transformation in my experiences has occurred. Blake once said that a fool who persists in his folly long enough will become wise. It is to folly or resistance that I therefore dedicate this work.

Acknowledgments

It is not possible to acknowledge everyone and everything that has contributed to the material here, other than to give credit to all who have gone before or have participated in the Collective Mind. Truth, which is universal, certainly precedes my interpretation. In that sense, what follows is original, though not necessarily original from me.

Still, special thanks is due Gary Leo Pedrosa for his general systems geometry that has provided insight and meaning to the mathematics of hermetica, and to my many friends who contributed encouragement and dialectic to the process of linguistically communicating much of what formerly I might have considered ineffable, experiential, and noetic.

The Author

Once a young man
Innocence aglow in his cheeks;
Stand still times' sand
While the shudder seeks.

Immortality created
In an image of light
Focused on film
Preserves the site.

Life takes its toll,
Etching from the soul lines that stray
From innocence aglow
To portraits of Dorian Gray.

Immortality created
In an image of light
Focused on film
Preserves the site.

Truth Is the Only Illusion
and/or
Questions on Enlightenment

Among the species of his world, man has a unique propensity to project and extrapolate his values upon "known" and "unknown" meanings having to do with his system of axiology, epistemology and metaphysics.

Man's basic value assumptions (axiology) predispose the nature of his knowing (epistemology) to such an extent that any ultimate "meaning" or "reality" quest (metaphysics) is circular or tautological by definition. Metaphysics, like science, often creates models and then sets about proving the models function from the perspective of the model's conformity with "knowns" (expectations).

Although models are useful constructs for the purpose of communicating unseen abstractions of observable events, they nevertheless necessarily say nothing about "reality." If one observes a mirage and recognizes it as such, is the sight of the mirage, or the mirage itself, the illusion? If consciousness is the force behind physical manifestation—and consciousness is in evolution seeking fulfillment—wherein exists the illusion?

In paradox or the dialetic process, one can *experience* the knowing that Webster defines as noetic. The experience is necessary to understanding. No amount of pure intellectual speculation will ever transcend itself. Synergism of knowing occurs from experience, which combines the energy of intellect with that of imagination (inspiration) and emotion.

Discursive intellect is inherently always limited to the boundaries of language and further handicapped by the assignment of meanings that are culturally positioned to orchestrate agreement.

What follows are the knots of pure intellectual reasoning that this author used to climb the rope of understanding. To many, the knots will not be obvious, as small knots in a line never are when viewed from a distance. Only upon close personal inspection can one view "irregularities" from the angle omitting assumption.

On Definitions

My postman friend Al once defined
a kiss as an anatomical
juxtaposition of two orbicularis oris
muscles in a state of contraction.

Isn't it wonderful that things are
not their definitions?

Pretending

Reality is a game we play
(or play at playing).
Some of us are better than
others at playing the game.
The rules of the game require
surrendering ourselves in order
to pretend to play ourselves.

Patterns

There comes a time (perhaps several over many lifetimes) when patterns emerge and conflict erupts. Conflict is resistance and resistance is fear. In selfishness one always harbors fear. I believe that the great unseen shackle is fear—more specifically, fear of rejection.

All of our defense mechanisms and compensation devices exist in order to preserve our image of okayness, acceptance, love and hate.

Hate separates us from ourselves. We hate what we fear. We are afraid *only* of rejection. We cannot love what we do not accept. What we condemn and run from diminishes each of us proportionately. In our fear, anger, and hatred is that which we inevitably become.

Patterns that lead us away from self-actualization, however they are manifest, are fear-based opportunities for learning. Learning in its highest sense is *always only* allowing (accepting, expressing) the unconditional gift of love that *is* each of us.

Why, Oh Y?

Tell me, tell me why,
Why is the sky so blue?
Or everything after a rain
Polished, glistening and new?

Tell me, tell me why,
Why do I seem to go through
Multi-dimensions of space and time
When I close my eyes—I still view?

Tell me, tell me why,
Why is there only a few
Who are genuinely concerned about
What can be said to be "really" true.

Tell me, tell me why,
Why is "knowing" what I always knew?
"Be still," the inner voice spoke silently,
"The Y in why is the first letter in you."

On Friends

All life is our friend if we approach
it in love, acceptance, and
friendship.
Each interaction with another
should take place as though
those involved were the last forms
of life on earth.

Ultimate Reality and Life

It's a process of being in and of
the process while
Revealing the Process.

The waters of consciousness
are within the vessel but not of
the vessel.

There are directions and elections
Not purpose and choice.

Seeing the Divine

When the emotionally
unacceptable is acceptable
the DIVINE has been seen.

On Stimuli

We may not be in charge of
certain stimuli
in our external environment,
but we definitely
are in charge of our
internal environment.

The Fruit of the Tree

Once upon a time a lowly man looked to himself. He spoke unto himself, "I desire to serve God, but my life has been full of sin. The example I have set is not that of a cleric. People will only scoff and say, 'Know ye them by the fruits of their tree.' Who am I then to speak for or of God?"

With these words circling within his head, the troubled man lay down to rest. He spoke to God, "Your will, not mine, be done."

As he drifted into sleep, pictures began appearing that told this story.

Once there stood a tree, a tree of life, full of fruit. The limbs bent toward the earth under the weight of the lush red cherries. The cherries danced in jubilee with the breeze that bathed their tender skins and turned their fullness and vivid color to face the Father, the Sun of the heavens.

With the dew and the rain they would polish their beauty and drink of the earth; to store within the energy and vitality of life taken from the soil through the roots and fired with the spirit of the Sun radiating through the leaves of their parent.

But alas, not all of the children of the tree would mature into lush red fruit. Out of an urge to experience and learn on his own, there was one that turned away from the Father and ignored the parental warnings. Charlie, as he was known by the others, kept his life juices warm, daring the cold, the frost, the elements. He began to fill with color and mature early.

Pivoting on his base, he turned away from the Sun and took shade in the leaves. Daring to fornicate with all the forms of the world, Charlie refused to release the natural pesticides within and took up affairs with the parasites.

Soon his delicate skin was broken and his fruit exposed. The fragrance attracted the birds and they too feasted on his flesh. Charlie lived of the flesh and of the world. Passion, experience, and knowledge were his prize.

Then one day the gardener came. Gently he took from the parent the pure and ripened children, leaving only Charlie behind. Hanging alone, Charlie looked about him. The fall nights were cold and lonely. His friends, the birds, were on wing abandoning him. His flesh had spoiled, and even the insects avoided him. His soul hung to his tattered body. The elements he once had faced with a thrill now threatened to snap him from the stem of life. Charlie was sad and lonely. He had learned these things: knowledge is not necessarily wisdom; experience is a teacher that is not always kind; and passion is sometimes a poison that betrays whatever value there is to be had in experience and knowledge.

Charlie looked up at the beautiful blue sky and the buoyant white pillowy clouds adrift, seemingly with nothing to do or a care in the world, lazily on sail across the vast blue heavens. "They and the lilies of the field," Charlie said unto himself.

"Dear God," he spoke aloud, "I have sinned. I have wasted the beauty of your flower and turned my back on simple truth. In my pursuit of wisdom, I lost sight of Your Great Form and indulged in physical illusions. I was lost. I alone am to blame. I give my essence over to thee, Creator of all that is good within me and all that could ever be love within me. For you *are* ETERNAL LOVE, and what is best for me is also your way. That I should discover this so late in my life is my most significant regret.

"I have watched the caterpillar spin his cocoon and perch on the leaves above me as a butterfly," Charlie continued, "but I fear that this chrysalis in my life has come so late that I will be unable to share *this Beauty, this Truth*, with others."

With that Charlie lowered his head. Suddenly a squirrel jerked him from the limb and scampered down the tree and across the meadow. The squirrel paused, examined Charlie, and then as though rejecting him, dropped and left Charlie behind in the grass.

Charlie rested there for a day or two and then the snow came. Covered by the white blanket, Charlie slept.

The seasons passed as though in the twinkling of an eye. Charlie took root and grew strong. From his branches came blossoms, followed by fruit more beautiful than Charlie could ever remember beholding.

Charlie praised and gave thanks to God!

Our lowly man raised his head from slumber. His prayer had been answered. The Lord does not forsake man; man forsakes the Lord. Thy will, not mine, be done; for, after all, in their eternal boundless beauty, they are one and the same.

On Victims

There are no victims
that are not victims of themselves.
Self-responsibility
sets one free of the
puppeteers' strings by empowering
the individual with the
capacity to be puppet
and puppeteer.
To the extent that self-power is
deferred by blame,
it is never within the
grasp of realization.

On "Fixers"

In your perfect self
all things are perfect.
Perfect yourself
and you
perfect the world.

On Teachers

We are all students,
teaching what we would
like to know.
The teacher's perfect pupil
is always him or herself.
There are no teachers,
for we are all
students.

On Ignorance

Ignorance precedes knowing.
To know is to love.
In ignorance there is less than love,
yet ignorance teaches love.
To the precise degree
we are ignorant,
we are that much less
than we could become.
What we could become is
who we really are.

On Clarity

To see all things clearly
is to see nothing.
Seeing clearly is looking upon
the invisible.
The visible world exists
because of the absence of clarity.
Rectification
is in the dual vision
of things and *no* things.
To give up everything
to obtain *no* thing is the
alchemy of discovery.

Discovery is remembering
and then practicing the "knowing"
as a learning
incorporated in the body.
When the body has learned,
the learning is complete.

On Education

We educate ourselves and our
children to lose ourselves,
to surrender our inner knowings,
to abandon our
imaginative powers;
in fact, to become absurd.

Where as education should seek
to remember,
it seeks to instruct.
Material learnings are lessons
in artifact history.
Courses in beingship
are pathways to mastery.
Mastery is service—
SERVICE TO SELF AND THE
COMMUNITY OF LIFE.
Any form of education
that would teach
otherwise does a disservice to the
intent of education.

Counterfeit Confetti

Label making:

> Prosperous
> Successful
> Competitive
> Autonomous and
> Independence

Goal achievement:

> Wealth
> Power
> Position
> Trophies and
> Experience.

Expense record:

> Family
> Friendship,
> Faith
> Fun and
> Innocence.

What cupid cotton candy concession—
Our contrived, counterfeit confections.
What a disastrous, devastating dilemma
In our avarice, carnivore reflections.

On the Material World

The particle
does not manifest itself
until observed.
Then the expectation
of the observer influences
the form of manifestation.
(Heisenberg's Uncertainty Principle).
So which came first,
the chicken or the egg?
The thought or the
physical manifestation?
Is there ever
one without the other?

On Reality Distinctions

We are all in some state of becoming human in the highest sense. All of our experiences contribute to who we are at the moment. Some experiences are imagined, hallucinated, confabulated, or dreamed, and some are those commonly referred to as "real." Thus, there exists a definition of real and synthetic experience and almost always an accompanying priority of relevance.

Relevance is found in the power of the experience and not the domain of distinction. A valid experience is one which contributes to good. The object of experience is the subject of learning. The experiences which subjectively contribute to a more loving, appreciative human contribute to all. When there is only love within, there is only love without.

On Problems

Problems exist only when
they are seen as obstacles.
Problems become opportunities
when viewed as
facilitators of learning.

Become What You Realize

Public prejudice dictates scarcity
While in a world *without* limitation;
In paradox consciousness slowly awakens:
Doubt inhibits the essence of realization.

Know only abundance and prosperity,
Acknowledge reality in Love and Light,
Transformation is in expression,
Thought forms the activity of Life.

On Consciousness

The particle world of *things* constitutes "reality" in classical western tradition. Yet all objects are different conglomerations of the same subatomic activity (wave form), which brings the physical into manifestation and paradoxically appears to require the nonmaterial action of consciousness. That is, the act of conscious observation and expectation manifests the wave as a particle. What then is *hard* science?

Science purports to investigate physical phenomena via "scientific method." Science appears to be investigating itself and pretending to investigate "reality."

Was the big bang the result of consciousness? Is history properly an account of consciousness as opposed to physical happenings? Are conscious events predecessors to physical "anythings"?

On Gratitude

All that one may ever become is a gift. Becoming is the process of being. Form and function are always synonymous. Change the way you think and you change your life.

Live in gratitude and you live in grace. Accept all in your life as a gift and know the peace that passeth understanding.

All that comes to one does so for some good. See the good in all and set yourself free. Begin each day with "Thank you, thank you, thank you," and meet each experience with the excited expectation, "I cannot wait to see what good comes from this."

To the Purpose of Life

To the purpose of life,
the mystery of strife,
the shadow of dark,
the voltage of light;
to black versus white,
the waste in our work,
come visions in the night—
Love is Life's Perfect Sight.

On Ego

Egos have power only when fed. No one has ever held an ego. Constructs may be helpful for understanding but necessarily say nothing about reality.

Resist something and you give it power. Do battle with an ego and watch it become more powerful. Attempting to overcome one's ego is like attacking windmills.

You are *one* person. Accept yourself as *whole* and you will become so. Divide yourself and be conquered by your illusionary divisions. Separateness does not exist within or without.

On I

Each of us has an "I" somewhere in our understanding of self. The "I" may even have a specific body location. The "I" is a representation of our illusion of separateness. The "I" is where hurt, grief, pain, joy, and fun take place mentally, to most at least.

The "I" is not as much a thing as a reference point. Just as two dots form or equal a straight line and the dots themselves are reference points, so the "I" is but a representation of some point of consciousness participating in an event that necessarily involves all consciousness.

Coin of the Realm

There is ultimately only one coin of the realm, and like all coins the sides are inseparable. This coin is more than a token of material success, for it represents the energy of eternal birthright.

Like all coins, its stored measure of wealth can be used to create additional stores of wealth. Invest it wisely and the Cosmos is yours.

So that you will recognize this coin when it comes into your life, a description of each side of the coin follows:

On one side are the words: "Whatever you do unto the least of thy brethren, you do unto me."

On the opposite side are the words: "Do unto others as you would have them do unto you."

When you hold this coin and invest its powers you will discover that it is minted from the bright white light of Universal Life and Love.

On God

God created *all* by first reflecting on Self, necessarily so since there was only God, and then dividing self; separating the firmaments from the heavens and so forth. All creation is a creation of God and is in the body of God just as surely as the cells of life forms are in the body of these life forms.

Just as a cell has the capacity to clone, or a tiny fragment of a holograph the inherent whole, all life (and *all* is life) is a representation of the whole, or God.

If one argues for limitation one will remain limited. Accept the Divine within and your perfect will, which is God's will, will be done.

On Lies

The greatest lie begins with a simple truth. There is no more compelling truth than the lie one desires to believe. Lies are sometimes easier to accept than truth—almost always so if the truth challenges a fundamental belief.

Fundamental beliefs arise from investment. Sacrifice is the sacredness of investment. What one has sacrificed sufficiently for one holds as important. The greater the sacrifice the more sacred that which was earned as a result.

Religion, politics, education, and science all have deferred gratification patterns, or sacrifice, which vests the practitioner with beliefs.

Being In Paradox

A wave of light taken from the string
Shapes the dimension of objects and things.
But shadows are illusory, truly no thing.
Then reality becomes a contingent nothing.

The particle is a wave form action
Observed in dependent reaction.
Independence apart from ego satisfaction?
A part of an "I ness", not "1 ness", faction?

Wholeness is *oneness* now here,
Nowhere is nothingness lacking despair.
In nothingness is being going nowhere.
In being in *oneness* all truly know where.

Where is always here and in *him*,
Ego in being is consciousness' only sin.
Does the intership of science seem dimmed?
Turn in; outward reality comes from within.

On "Knowing"

The shadow cannot reflect
upon the form.
As a reflection,
it inherently lacks
the ability to understand itself
through *only* self.

On Sacred Geometry

The most sacred verse
ever written
is that which *is* the world.
Thoughtful observation of nature
reveals the
geometry of meaning.
The discovery of patterns
unveils the lesson
of the moment
every time.

I Am That I Am

In God's work,
Or the Will that is behind it,
Is your work
And the Will of your inheritance.

In harmony
The two are One,
Creating a symphony
Of Eternal Love.

Lose not the sight
of one with the ONE,
And all things are added:
The "am" in I AM, becomes.

On Power

Power surrounds necessity.
Necessity is illusion.
Necessity this and necessarily that
breeds otherness — separateness,
punishment and reward are born.

God only LOVES.
GOD IS LOVE.
All that is or may become
is an unconditional gift
of love.
Emulating this LOVE
is the process fueling
all learning.
The temporal world
exists only to learn.

On Reason

Reason is the 20/20 hindsight
that prides itself
on explaining experience.
Experience is the
dog and reason is its tail.
For some,
the tail often wags the dog.

Trusting one's experience
is the first step
toward achieving insight.
Insight is limited
only to the imagination.
As there is a body,
mind, and spirit,
so there is emotion,
intellect, and imagination.
Experience
is the simultaneous occurrence
of all without the
interference of reason.

All I May Become

My Dearest Father,
it is your presence within
That is truly I,
And my presence in You
That is all I may become.

On Perception

I see a mirage. I know it is a mirage. What is faulty—the observed (mirage) or the observer? Is the illusion (maya) like the mirage? Or is it dependent upon the psychological needs of the observer? Is there any real difference?

Perhaps my thinking doesn't change the world, but it changes my world. My world is always dependent upon my perception—not the other way around.

There are people playing in the mirage. They do not realize it is all a mirage, an illusion. I think I'll play at playing in the mirage while I observe my playing.

On Coincidence

There is no such thing
as coincidence.
Occurrences knit themselves
together in a
tapestry of synchronicity.
Accidents are
serendipitous events
providing opportunity.

Of Matter

Each day is born in contradiction,
For every positive there exists a negative
And for every energy there exists a mass,
Resting on the continuum is Man in interdiction.

Tomorrow promises that someday
Our understanding will antiquate our sorrow,
That the real promise of tomorrow one day
Is the certain promise of no tomorrow.

Alternative

To be or not to be;
in the alternative:
to be *and* to be.
Observed and observer as one.
Why not?
It looks like fun.

On Inspiration

Inspiration occurs from either the awe of beauty or the frustration of limitations. Inspiration is a manifestation of the creative energy of imagination or spirit. It is the fuel that can and will propel the passenger in any direction. Whatever one imagines one begins to create. The more emotional that which is imagined, the more complete the creation and thus the more rapidly it is manifest.

Energy is energy. You decide its polarity. You are the pilot and the passenger. It is just as easy to imagine in love or from reverence as it is to create from fear and anger.

On Reverence

There is beauty in *all!*
Reverence
is the act of beholding
beauty.

A Message to You

A spotted fawn pokes out its head
And bravely dares the aspen edge;
The rodent raises from out its hole,
Their eyes exchange an innocent role.

The dew has moistened the wooded green,
It glistens bright with a polished sheen.
The yellow rays reflect upon the forest floor
Extending life's gift from heaven's door.

A covenant to mankind, a prism of color,
Descending to caress the bosom of its mother.
The envelope closes, leaving only twinkling light,
Appearing in the distance is the chariot of night.

Drifting in flight above the mountain high,
Silhouetted by the dawn, soft shadows in the sky.
Reflecting below on a blue mirror of nature
The rushing falls are stilled in a blending rapture.

The symphony provided by God-given beauty
Inspires the orchestra to a much higher duty;
This bouquet of bounty is but a shy attempt
At returning what love has meant.

On Phenomena

When you discern the difference between the container and the contents you will know reality. Reality transcends the finite explanations discovered and rediscovered by mankind. Phenomena is the occurrence of reality taking place at a point in time and space that is less formalized than the paradigms referred to as "reality."

In the phenomena (true phenomena) exists the opportunity to see the same thing differently. Science has always held genius out as that mind that sees differently. Truth exists in the anomalies man cannot understand. After all, how could the finite explain the infinite?

On Futility

A soft powder blue depth surrounds
The jagged apertures that thrust upward
Into the transparent visible blue sky.
Its color portrays an end, a wall,
A painted finish out there somewhere
Where everything had to "really" begin.

To end is to begin—to begin is to end.
To choose is to choose not.
To act is to fail to act.
To will, to act, to anything
Is to choose and thereby to choose not.

I remember a childhood story
About a tiger who chased his tail.
How silly that he should chase his tail
Or fail to realize that the path
Of his demise was in his pursuit.

On Purpose

Purpose *is* the illusion.

As there is no time—there exists no purpose.

The natural *is*. You *are!* Being *is* becoming—causes, purposes, crusades are conditional. Being is unconditional! Being is eternal. Being is naturally natural.

With the blessing of intellect came confusion. From the fruit of the tree of knowledge arose the unnatural.

Knowledge is not wisdom. In paradox one finds equilibrium. Thesis to antithesis culminating in synthesis.

Allow, and being unfolds naturally. Allow respect for self and all!

Perceptions: A Tautology

There exists the absence of perception
Which implies the presence of perception.
There exists then perception of something
Communicated by perception of the perceived something.
The perceived something's perception is contingent
On the qualified perceptual abilities of the perceiver.
Qualification of the perceiver consists of agreement
Among perceivers whose perception generally agrees.
Agreement is a derivative of social education
And thus, perception is an approximation of preconception!

There Are *No* Losers

There is only now.
In the moment of now all exists.
One plays a game
and pretends past and future.
Players claim victory and defeat.
What occurs does so because it is.

You *is*, I *is*
exactly where we are
"supposed" to be.
We learn or evolve in our
understanding of *is*ness
by accepting,
allowing and loving.

Reflections on Mr. Buber

The experience of perception is not
Equal to the perception of "experience,"
And the sphere of reality relates
Only to the reality of our sphere;
Then the crisis of our environment
Delimits the dimension of our difference,
And the difference in our dimensions
Destructs the existence of "experience."

Service is Selfish

A Master realizes that the law of the universe yeilds tenfold from what one sows. Each act of altruism yields dividends beyond comprehension. What then is altruism?

Service is an act of joy. One engages in service simply because it is fun! Whatever one stores or does not store exists only in retrospect. The motive in true service is selfish: purely and simply joy and fun.

Service without joy is duty. Duty is conditional. Conditionality cannot by definition be eternal.

Wisdom

Wisdom is knowing what one does not know,
Realizing what cannot be said to be known,
Investigating the options of knowing,
Unearthing the fallacies of truth while
Embracing the absence of knowledge,
And then postulating on the presence of Reality.

On Confusion

Free will (choice)
is a product of confusion.

When wisdom exists,
clarity prevails.
In clarity there is no alternative.
Alternatives arise
only when confusion suggests
an either/or possibility.

On Opposites

Polarity is the glue
of the universe.
Without opposites
there exists *no* thing
known in the physical.
Opposition
is an inherent energy
to polarity.
Only in the midpoint
of opposites does balance exist.

Resistance is always opposition.
In balance there is
nothing to resist.

On Agency

Being in the physical presupposes action. Agency without action is not possible in a world of birth and decay, energy becoming mass, unconscious motives hidden from conscious thoughts, and so forth.

Since action is therefore necessarily implied, the only question is one of "right" action, and yet all acts occur because that is exactly what was supposed to occur. *What* is supposed to occur? An opportunity for learning. Learning will occur. History does repeat itself.

On Unconditional Love

Unconditional love
is the absence
of expectation.

An Acorn Without an Oak

To have loved, as has been said,
From afar—pure and chaste of heart,
Is to witness the world without senses, or
To behold the heavens absent of stars.

On Compatibility

Compatibility
is based on common
emotional needs.
Emotion does not respond
to reason.

For Every Anger Response There Exists Fear

The nature of fear is resistance. What one resists he becomes. What one represses he eventually acts out. Love is indeed no more or less than eliminating fear. Anger is simply *A Nasty Getting Even Response*. Fear and anger perpetuate one another in a vicious cycle. With each fear/anger response the cycle rate increases, creating intensity to sometimes seemingly inescapable circularity.

Acceptance is joy! Approval is conditional—conditional to this or that. Love is unconditional!

On one end of the calculus exists acceptance and joy and at the other end is fear and anger. All negative emotions arise from fear/anger while the peace that passeth understanding dwells in acceptance/joy (unconditional love).

Bless what might trigger your ire and enjoy the blessings of peace "within," irrespective of the stimuli of the environment "without."

On Agreements

Agreements
have expectations.

Love Lost

All in all,
When I assess
The life we
Shared together,
I realize that
All the good,
The growth and
Love, lasts forever.

Along the way
We helped a few
And learned about
Life's real treasures.

Yes, all in all,
I'd do it over
Despite the pain
Of tomorrows severed.

So, soar my love,
For I've let go
Of all the lines
That once tethered.

You are free
To fly away—
To stretch your wings,
To search and discover.

But, all in all,
You should know
You were a gift—
I'd do it over!

On Infinity

Infinity has meaning
only in time and space.

On Dimensions

Dimensions overlay perception.
Perception optionalizes dimensions.

On Love

To the extent
that one diminishes another—
he diminishes himself;
and yet, paradoxically,
one cannot give
what one does not have
to give.
Therefore, love yourself
and you can love others;
love others so you can
love yourself.

On Fear

Love is
the abandonment of fear.
Fear is
the selfish want of love.
I want this, I want that,
I need this, and so on.

I need . . .
is fear speaking.

On Sacrifice

Love is the process
of giving oneself up
for the gain of another,
but sacrifice is not Love.
In Love,
the giving to someone else
is receiving
the gift yourself.

Contracts are agreements,
and agreements
are based upon what each gets
out of the contract.
Love is based upon
what one puts into it.

A Fairy Tale

Once upon a time a young boy fled from his home into an unknown jungle. William Hurt, or Will as everyone called him, felt unloved by his family and friends. Bright and stubborn, fearful and angry, Will ran and ran so far into the jungle that he lost himself.

The jungle became a maze. Will wandered in circles, surviving on what he could take from the jungle. Will studied the animals and began to model their behavior. The jungle seemed to survive only for the fittest. Will thought, "The last one to starve is the tiger."

Will became more and more like the beasts he came to admire. They were tough, aggressive, and unafraid. Will desired more than anything else to be unafraid. Day after day he acted the role of the beast, sometimes believing himself, "I am unafraid."

Will observed the beast roar and the jungle tremble. Will began to roar. As his roars became louder and louder, he began to believe them . . . he was unafraid.

One evening while Will reflected on his battles and conquests, victories taken by the strength of his roar and the unmerciless cunning of his mind, a Fairy Princess appeared before him. She was bright with the glory of dew drops on a summer morning. She shined and sparkled like the forest after a polishing rain. Her presence was as pure as the morning air. Long, flowing dark hair framed a face more beautiful and radiant than Will had ever dreamed.

The Fairy Princess offered to lead Will out of the jungle. She was so breathtaking that he agreed to follow. And follow he did, though the trek was over unknown ground that sometimes frightened Will. The princess was patient even when Will roared to conceal his fear.

Along the way, with a map for Will to follow, the Fairy Princess turned herself into gold, so much gold that the earth was covered with shiny coins. She promised Will that the gold was so valuable that it would make him rich beyond his imagination.

Will was unfamiliar with gold. The coins filled his pockets and overflowed his pack. In time, as Will struggled in his journey out of the jungle, the gold became heavy. The weight seemed to slow his stride. Will remembered how fleet the beast must be to survive. Will trusted the Fairy Princess and didn't want to let go of any of the gold coins. Still, torn as he was between her promise and his survival learning, Will panicked and started to run.

His lope was awkward, his speed was slow, and as he ran the coins began to bounce out of his pack. As the load lightened Will began to roar, afraid to stop and unable to run, and he roared so loud that the pack he carried fell to the ground. His stride lengthened and his fear expanded as he raced to the edge of the jungle.

Finally, before him stood the most exquisite place he had ever beheld. He stopped, breathless and fearful. Now Will realized that he was also afraid to leave the jungle. No roaring was allowed outside the jungle.

Will worried, "What if I lose the gold? How would I survive?" The magic land before him had no predators. The jungle, at whose edge he now stood, was at least familiar. Will paced back and forth on the apron of the jungle and the magic land. He had to make a decision between fears, and all he was able to do was roar.

Nightfall came and Will lay down exhausted. He tossed and turned. The coin in his pockets became like rocks on the ground, so Will emptied his pockets and fell back asleep.

The sun rises in the east and Will opened his eyes just in time to see its glory rising on the horizon. The brightness provided Will with courage. He stood up and entered the magic land.

Will walked straight to the city gates. There he stood looking through the bars at the joy inside. Children played while couples embraced. Dogs chased one another in a game of tag while squirrels ate out of people's hands. The lion lay down with the lamb.

The city was a place of pure love. All that abided within were beings of love. There existed no fear, no judgment, no anger, no greed. The inhabitants of the city were at peace with themselves and the world around them.

Will began to weep. His shame and guilt for all that he had preyed upon while in the jungle flashed before him. His heart was heavy with sadness.

He lay at the gate too ashamed to entreat entrance. Sorrow overcame him. The greatest treasure on earth lay before him and he denied his own entrance out of shame.

The night was long, but the sun also rises. With dawn rose a new Will. "Life," Will claimed, "provides the opportunity to set things right." Will pledged to hold his head high and to serve others. Will realized that service to others was the highest service to self. Will "knew" that his fear had been unfounded. Will also knew that fear devours love. What he had hated—fear itself—had deprived him of experiencing anything but fear. His fears had rejected trust; his anger had violated peace; his roar had fooled only himself.

Will approached the gates to the enchanted city. He tried to open their pink hinges, but to no avail. The gates were locked. He called forth into the city and a gatekeeper approached.

Will was taken back. The gatekeeper was like a mirror reflection of himself. Will spoke only after a long stare. "I would like to reside in your city."

"It takes gold to open the gates. Do you have gold?" the gatekeeper responded.

"Gold?" Will questioned.

"This is the land of love. Only honor, peace, harmony, and balance abide here. The gold I speak of is Love. Where is your gold?" replied the gatekeeper.

Will reached into his pockets; they were empty. "The gold . . . where is the gold?" raced through Will's mind. He turned and ran back to the edge of the jungle. His heart would not stop pounding as he frantically searched for the gold.

Days passed and Will could find no gold. He cried out, "Oh, Fairy Princess, where is the gold?" A voice spoke from afar: "The gold is gone."

Will's heart sank. He lamented, "How could I be so foolish? How could I be so selfish, so thoughtless, so fearful?"

"Please, Fairy Princess," Will pleaded, "I love you so! Please, Fairy Princess, there must be some remaining gold."

"There is no gold," the voice responded, "there is no gold. You ran so fast that most of me fell away from you. What was left, you placed on the ground like common stones and walked away."

Will could not believe his senses. This couldn't be true. "Fairy Princess," he spoke, "you are the gold. You are here now. I can hear your voice and sense your shadow. I know you can reappear. You *are* gold! Gold can and will return your strength, honor, and courage. You gave me your gold. I did not lose it all. I will return enough gold to you for both of us to enter the enchanted city. . . . Look into my heart Fairy Princess, do you see the gold?"

"Yes I do, Will Hurt."

"Then I freely give you all of my gold. What will you do, Fairy Princess? Will you take the gold . . . will you accept my love . . . will you abandon your fear or will you refuse my gold? What will you do, Fairy Princess?"

This is a fairy tale. Any story that begins with once upon a time always ends happily.

What if it were not a fairy tale? Even Princesses (and Princes) have fears. Why not dare to risk and show your love to the one you care about most today.

The Death of Love

There is no death of Love,
Although transitions may come
And angry hearts push and shove—
Until Love's feelings finally numb.

There is no loss or sorrow,
Except that fear turns the power
Of all the promises of tomorrow
Into the desolation of the Tarot Tower.

Love never withers and dies,
But rejection often sets aside
All the beauty shared, in gasping sighs
Of empty dreams where loneliness resides.

Love lives eternal lives where
Time and loss know no "truth"
And higher selves forever share
The biblical love portrayed by Ruth.

The Force

Love is a force; the surgeon's scalpel is an instrument. Instruments all have inherent within them a use and misuse application.

Forces, like all energy forms including instruments, possess by application both use and misuse principles.

Love can divide countries and motivate war. Love possesses or frees.

Man is the fulcrum—the user—that through his intention applies usage principles and practices that pervert or transcend.

Man himself is both force and tool. He is experimenter and the experiment. His definition of right and wrong, magical and sinful are his blueprints for the artifacts of illusion. Man is, in truth, truth itself. He cannot create truth or explain truth, for that is like the shadow explaining the form. Fulfillment is being natural and the natural is the magical.

On Resolution

Choice is only an illusion
Arising purely from some confusion;
Leading straight to disillusion;
Denying fruition and resolution.

Woman

In all of nature
Perfection abounds,
In manifest glory
Crystal is found.

Filling its matrix.
Light underground
Raises triumphantly
Wonder—profound!

As brilliant as crystal
Each facet a fire,
Spectacular in energy as
When love is desire.

The radiance of a woman
Her giving vibrant as the lyre
Ascends to the heavens, a
Crystal in the One's attire.

On Marriage

Symbols are outward manifestations of inner reality. Behavior (conduct) is a symbol system. Conduct in a marriage is the system of the partners. Conduct affects the system first as the system affects the conduct.

Only the wise marry understanding that *all* of one's behavior should first be based on the needs of one's partner.

Giving oneself entirely to his partner ensures that his partner has something to give in return.

Giving first to self only guarantees that a partner will eventually begin giving only to himself. One cannot receive what he does not give.

Personal Love

Love is sometimes like a ship
at sea—
There is no ocean voyage
storm free.

On Fidelity

The virtue of absolute fidelity is in the bonding of mature love. The closeness shared by and between one couple in love blooms only when their sexual relations are held sacred.

The giving over of oneself entirely to another is manifest in the inviolate nature of total and unselfish commitment and trust.

Sex outside of marriage is selfish and manifests only selfishness. Open sex is no more than a defense mechanism that incorporates the fear of rejection into the relationship by denial, and thus the open marriage, and/or is a brutal act against self, loved one, and relationship.

Relationships are risking. Risking is love. Enduring love risks all by giving self over completely to the other.

Antithesis

The moon shown full
Beneath the pillowed gray,
While the nights immersed
The terror that would fray
At the tinsel of thread
Between living and dead.

Horror lurks beneath that moon, and
Children sing of the dish and the spoon
While young hearts beat in romantic bloom.

Nursery rhymes sing to the mind
Of innocent days long gone by,
Cradled behind Mother Goose
Playful characters on the fly
Trek across a heaven of blue
While the cat and the dog jump over the moon.

Children sing of the dish and the spoon
Young hearts beat in romantic bloom
While horror lurks beneath the moon.

Softly wrapped by each other
And embraced by heaven's stars,
Legendary Luna kindles
Fanciful tenderness from afar
With romance excited by expectation
And unaware of Antithesis mitigation.

Young hearts beat in romantic bloom,
Horror lurks beneath the moon
While children sing of the dish and the spoon.

On Forgiveness

Forgiveness is an act, not just a state of mind. Genuine forgiveness *is* Divine simply because one must put himself at risk to forgive.

Speaking "I forgive" is like an introduction. Living "I forgive" is opening oneself up to a relationship that history may suggest to be painful.

Forgiveness in personal love relationships is the opportunity to genuinely express that love.

There is never true forgiveness without risk, just as there is never personal love without an opportunity to forgive.

On the Past

To be sovereign is to be alone.
To be threatened is to be alone.
To feel grief, sorrow, anguish or guilt,
To share passion, lust, and even love;
To recall—is to be alone.

Saddened that a memory lives
And yet is dead.
Bereaved that the paths have not always
Lead straight ahead: for many—
I wish were dead.

Tomorrow beckons new approaches
And promises horizons filled with content.
Still I remember past franchises
Perverted somehow to leave only contempt
Yet tomorrow the promise will somehow be kept.

How shallow the momentum
From which life must flourish.
How calloused a heart must be to heal.
How much must be shared to finally be alone,
And how lonely it is to reflect on that which we have known.

On Guilt

"What is guilt?" queried the seemingly bewildered young man.

Where does it come from and what must I do to understand?

Does it run rampant from the manner in which I am tutored as a child?

Or is there some immutable law whose system should never be defiled?

How do I know when what I feel is a justified form of guilt?

And how do I prove that there really is something lurking—like guilt?

Tell me, why doesn't all of mankind suffer its pangs, given the same source?

After all, shouldn't there be some common rudiment directing its course?

The old man unctuously stared as he pondered upon the young man.

But there was only silence as time was recorded by the grains of sand.

Young man, I hesitate to answer when you come before me extending your hand.

Hoping to grip at some vestal vestige of unadulterated truth,

When all I can give you is the innocence of understanding you had in your youth.

All the wisdom that can be learned as time paces one's rhythm toward decay,

Will teach you only that all in the world is by nature a passing parade.

There can be no persevering finite structure emancipated as the anatomy of truth,

Only a vanquish or betrayal which comes privately when we have fostered a personal "untruth."

If your heart dictates a wanton fear of quiet guilt or pain.

It is only because you participate in parcelling out some other's ill fame.

In the virginity of youth we created an aura of genuineness and love,

Then, mitigated by our maturing faculties—we cast the dust of coal on a pure white dove.

The Whole Human

There exists mind, body, and spirit. To mind is intellect, to body the physical, to spirit the unlimited power of the imagination.

To suppress imagination as an invalid experience is to deny experience of the spirit.

There exists three components of the unevolved: Love, Nowness and Trancendence. Love cancels the need to control anyone or anything. Living in the ever present *only* now eliminates fears that somehow security, which is never an out-there proposition but always found ultimately within, will be taken from one. Transcendence reduces sensation and/or sensate drives to the common denominator of happiness—peace within. In this state of peace, sensation becomes an inner awareness experience transforming the addiction for outer feeling stimuli.

In the mysticism of the twelve-pointed star the interfaces can be seen as two six-pointed stars set at angle one from the other:

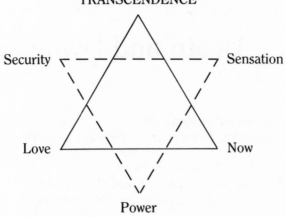

TRANSCENDENCE

Security — Sensation

Love — Now

Power

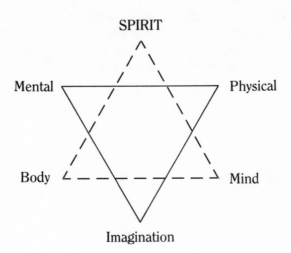

SPIRIT

Mental — Physical

Body — Mind

Imagination

Death and Dying

Living is the beginning of dying. Death is a mortal word and mortality is illusion. Nothing in the fabric of the Universe is ever lost.

Transformation from the physical to the metaphysical is only a shift in attention. The focus of physical this and that becomes, like shifting our gaze from left to right, the immersion of awareness in the totality of love.

The transformation process from carnate to incarnate, on and on, is neither more nor less than changing vehicles in a long journey homeward bound.

The journey only ends when we choose that our lessons have culminated in examination and our self-appraisal accepts our grade. We create the journey, the examination, and the grade. It is our awareness that the Father unconditionally loves which gives rise to our process of emulating that love. Therein lies the process behind the journey.

A Journey

I have had many thoughts go through my mind over the past two weeks. I have formed the opinion that fear and love are opposite emotions. Analogously, it is as if I fill a cup full of coffee and then decide to add cream. Some coffee will be displaced. I will displace as much coffee as I allow cream to be added. If we see love in this human condition as the ability to perceive some good in all things, and the ability to care about others before we care about ourselves (in the words of Christ, "Do unto others," love others as though they were ourselves); if we perceive love in this way, as we see in our analogy with the coffee cup, to the extent that I hold fear I displace a certain amount of love. It is my opinion that I have had many bogiemen in my own life. I have been frightened of many things. And at the same time I have not been frightened. Let me digress for a moment. I am a private investigator, criminologist, and as a child growing up I was a tough kid on the block. An acquaintance once made fun of me and embarrassed me about cigarette smoking. There was a certain disapproval and rejection in his words. I was extremely annoyed, and told the individual I smoked because I liked smoking. When he persisted, I took hold of his hand and put my cigarette out in his palm. That is a negative example of the analogy —fear converts itself to anger and displaces our ability to love.

I was once told by an informant of mine, a half-black retired professional boxer, that I had a street name, and that street name was Buffalo Balls. I was proud of that for a long time, since what he was conveying to me was the idea that as far as everyone on the street was concerned I was absolutely reckless when it came to matters of courage. I would run in where, as the saying goes, angels dared not tread. I can look upon that now, as I did the earlier experience related here (and many others in my life), as an act of total cowardice. What I have discovered about myself is that in order to conceal my fears I had to act courageously, and the definition of that in our western world is the act of some John Wayne, macho, fill your hands you sons of bitches model.

You see, what I am suggesting is sort of a formula or, shall we say, lesson in love. It is based on the earlier premise that these two opposite emotions—

love and fear—inhibit one another. In other words, if you would like only anger and hostility in your life, eliminate love and recognize everything fearfully. Unfortunately, most of us do this at a subconscious level or as a part of our enculturation process. We have loaded guns at our beds in the event that a criminal should enter the premises unlawfully while we sleep. We anticipate difficulty when we see a motorcycle gang ride into our proximity. We look for opportunities to express our courage and, possibly due to our fear, we may actually set up a reality. To the extent that we fear something, we usually have an ability to manifest it; that is, if I fear sufficiently contracting a disease, if I dwell on it for prolonged periods, I will convince myself that I have that disease. I will even convince those around me that there is something dreadfully wrong here. It is a set of circumstances much like we are familiar with in the saying that animals have an ability to sense fear in human beings. Those who are fearful are often bitten. Not only is this true, but in a very real physical sense we can and do attract exactly unto us as the mental movie maker projects. I can remember Boone's marvelous book, *Letters to Strong Heart*, wherein he spoke of rattlesnakes. These rattlesnakes never bit the Indians, but when the white men came the snakes seemed to have a delightful interest in biting them. It is in our ability to see ourselves as separate, as uniquely other than the rest of the world, that we become in fact other than all things in the world. To that extent we minimize our optimum reality.

Christ said the kingdom of heaven is here and now, that his Father had many mansions. You and I are mansions. We are in a physical plane. In this physical plane we often opt to see it as a sort of punishment/reward system. Not many of us begin our days by thanking someone or something for that day. As a matter of fact, a good friend of mine has said that when you ask people how many begin their day by the simple words *thank you*, you often get some very perplexed looks. More often than not there are comments like "Thank you for what?" Yet, if these same people who are saying "thank you for what?" were asked, "What would you do in your life if you had only two more days to live?" they certainly would tell you about many changes that they would make.

Well, each day that we live is an opportunity to live in heaven. Heaven is here and now. It always has been—but so has hell. We limit our reality, or the acceptance of our reality—our heaven here and now—and we limit it primarily with this function of other and this after thought of fear and its collective group of associated emotions.

Let me return to what I mean by the act of absolute cowardice, and the purpose behind my journey to the desert. You see, as we look at courage and act out courage, when we act it out in this John Wayne mentality that I alluded to earlier, we set ourselves up as uniquely other and against the world. There are guys in black hats and there are guys in white hats. Some of us get our courage in the hat colored black; some of us get our courage in the hat colored white. Because I have fears—personal, secret fears, bogiemen so to speak—I convinced myself that I am really brave. In order to be so, I must act bravely in the world, to stand where others cower. It is not to be timid. Now, I do not mean to suggest that there is no such thing as right action; in fact, with right action, as Ghandi said, there is absolute duty that attends it. What I am talking about is attitudes, and how our attitudes develop the exclusiveness we call ego that separates us from the rest of the world, that separates us from our loved ones, that separates us from ourselves.

I will confess one of my weaknesses. Years ago, for some reason or other (I have often attributed it to seeing the movie *Psycho*, and since then have learned of subliminals that were used in this movie to heighten fear and to stick these fears in the subconscious mind) I developed a childish fear of showering. When showering with my eyes closed, particularly when shampooing my hair, I have been fearful that someone would enter the bathroom. Something—ghost, goblin, perhaps that little girl from the *Exorcist* whose head spun as she vomited over the priest—would be sitting there on the toilet, or perhaps I would open my eyes and she would be sitting there in the shower with me. These fear thoughts brought chills that made me uncomfortable, uncomfortable enough that at times I have attempted to shampoo my hair without closing my eyes. Anything I could look at I felt comfortable with, but if I could not see it, if it might sneak up somehow and surprise me or overwhelm me in some sense of the word, it was relegated to a category of the spooky.

I have had other fears. I had fears that someone would break into my home and stab me in the middle of the night. I had fears that I would be somewhere with a woman that I wanted to impress and a gang of tough guys would come onto the scene and humiliate and embarrass me. I had fears about sounds and noises I heard in the dark of the night. I often felt forced to turn on a light so I could *see* from whence they came. I was always comfortable if there were people around me. If I shared a space, even the bathroom where I showered with my wife while she combed her hair, I was comfortable. But when I was all alone I had to contend with these secret demons, these fears.

Now, in coming to understand myself, I realize that these are fears that I have taken out into my world, and that these fears force me to act "courageously." (Let's put that word in quotation marks, for you see, this is sort of dribble-down effect.) Each of you have your own fears too. Deception— for example, an innocent comment that is not strictly the truth—is an act of fear. Why else would there be a lie? If I tell someone that I spent "x" amount of dollars on the town, did I exaggerate how many dollars I spent on my evening out because I want to feel important or because I fear that they will not perceive me as important? Whenever one lies, whether it is a petty lie or important lie (if such a difference should be made at all), one does so out of fear.

Well, let us consider the other emotions, those things that are not acts of our better, higher selves. When I am angry, I am angry out of fear. Even when I am angry at an associate, or, for that matter, anyone else who has not seemed to understand the instructions I have given them, in actuality I am afraid. Obviously, I do not fear them physicially and I do not fear their ability or inability to discharge the duties I have given them. I fear some consequence that may come as a result of their failure. Perhaps in some instances I am just feeling a little bit insecure, and so by acting out the dominance role of our western male and thoroughly throttling someone who made a mistake, I am demonstrating my superiority. Again, an absolute act of cowardice or fear.

Now, fear in this sense is different from being fearful. Fear is usually limited to a more narrow definition. The fear I speak of is much different from what is felt when we see one of our children at the edge of a river, acting in a manner that causes fear of their imminent drowning. That fear is for the life of the child, and if we scold the child afterward, it is usually in the embrace of our arms. We are so glad that the child was saved, that we were there to be a party to saving him and even in our great anger and fear over that situation we are showering the child with love and attention. But if I should take this same situation and eliminate the love and attention, I have created an act of cowardice. I have created or participated in an act of selfishness or a practice of one-upmanship. The game of one-upmanship itself is cowardice, for whenever I try to make myself better than someone else I have powered the notion of difference, and when I have powered that notion of difference, I have set up a situation for fear. If I take pride in being better, more intelligent, possessing certain credentials, acquiring lots of money, becoming affluent, or having a better sense of judgment, I take power away from others. And when I do this, what happens when I start to lose it? If I lose any of it I become less than that which I took pride in, and when this happens, I begin to act out the emotions of fear. Perhaps I become angry with people, angry with situations or conditions, or I become jealous. How many times have we seen someone become successful and someone else will say, "Oh, he is lucky." Or, "he inherited his wealth." Or, "he was born with a silver spoon in his mouth and has had good cobblestones under his feet all of his life." For, to recognize that the person has done anything better, worked harder, tried with more diligence, or desired with a greater sense of the word than we have desired, is to accept a measure of defeat for ourselves and to accept something that is less than we would like to perceive about ourselves, or to rationalize that we really did not care much about it after all.

Few people take the position that life is whatever they make of it. Most of us believe that for various reasons there are certain limitations on what we can and cannot do. But limitation is not a natural law; limitation is a self-imposed process. We convince ourselves and are convinced by society and those around us that anything that we may do in this world is limited by our ability to do it. So it takes money to make money, and yet there are stories of millionaires who began with nothing. So it takes education, a college degree, to become successful, and yet there are many stories of the uneducated who have become successful.

I have often wondered what would happen if Christ came to the earth again, gathered a crowd in one of the major parks, and began to practice what he practiced when he was on this earth before. He would be arrested, of course. He would not have a license to gather an assembly of that type. The medical association would certainly want him locked up, for he would be healing people, practicing medicine without a license. There would be a good deal of spiritual quandary, and there would be various churches who would say he is teaching heresy. It would be no different today than it was then; in fact, I have been told by a close friend of mine who possesses many psychic powers that Christ *has* been back to this earth on many occasions since the crucifixion and that the world was not ready for him.

As I look at the realities that influence my own life, I begin a journey. I will continue to record the journey just as I am recording this introduction to the journey. You see, I am going into the desert, of which I know nothing. I have deliberately avoided reading anything about the desert. I could not tell one cacti from another. I am aware that there are snakes, spiders of various species, and a variety of other bugs. There are even small predators. It would be an unfair test if I were to go to the mountains, because I would be completely comfortable in the mountains. In general, I would know how to survive, because I have been trained to survive in the mountains. But I know nothing of the desert, nothing whatsoever. In order for me to release my fears, to learn these lessons in love, I must remove myself from wherever there might be a light switch, from whatever support system makes me comfortable. I feel that in my own particular, unique instance, this is the way I can come to deal with fear. I have come to understand that if I can look fear straight in the face, if I can take the most fearful thing in the world —the dragon that wakes me in the middle of the nightmare—put my arms around it and give it love, it will either cease to exist or will return my love. If I can give it love, really give it love, it will disappear, and nothing fearful remains.

So, I plan to take my fears and go to the desert where I know nothing. I sever myself from various umbilical cords. I will travel with a friend, who will leave me in the desert and who will relieve me of most of my possessions. I will have no identification. I will have no wealth with me. I will take only the clothes I wear. I have brought with me a canteen which I will fill, and a supply of nuts and dried fruits. I know not how long I will be in the desert. With no other support system and nothing but wilderness desert around me, I will learn to deal with the fears that I carry with me every day, that I have imposed upon others in my cowardly commissions of courage. I will learn to embrace those fears, to love reality in all things, to see it in its proper perspective.

I have the feeling I may come back a babbling idiot. A friend has said that his mother raised a fool, not a flipping idiot. Perhaps my mother raised both in me. This will be the record of that journey. I have chosen the desert around Joshua Tree National Monument. There is a vortex of sorts there known to many people. An interruption in the ordinary electromagnetic function of our world as we know it. There, it is alledged, are many holy places, spiritual places, sacred to the Indians. I have chosen this area, for I realize that of myself I cannot overcome anything. It is the higher me, the higher self, the presence of the Father within that will do the battle. I will simply turn affairs over to him. Without that understanding, the trip would be absolutely meaningless, a contest with all that I would encounter, a test of the fittest. Survival of the fittest is not to be the test. If the snake senses that I am different, it will bite me. If the coals at the bottom of my feet are separate, I will be burned. But as any master who walks on coals would tell you, the secret is in the fact that there is no distinction.

I suppose I should look forward to it, like going home, becoming one with those things I will encounter, threatening nothing, giving love to all. And yet, I must admit that there would be no need for the journey if I were not fearful. As a doctor of metaphysics, I have told many people there is no law of limitation, no good and evil in battle, only large gaps in our perception of reality and (this on many occasions) that reality, whether as examined in a particle accelerator on a sub-atomic level or from the perspective of the ancient texts of the Qabalah and the Vedas or as modern metaphysicians refer to the universal laws of the equity, karma, abundance, that all these flow in meaning and substance only from understanding the first principle — God is not good and evil. God is only good; we are creatures of light and love. Within us exists a sort of "gene" and if we properly stimulate that gene, we can clone a perfect capacity for being God-like. In that sense we can manifest in the real world, to the glory of the Father, a place or path of understanding, a kingdom of God here and now. We are holograms of God and in God. All that we can ever be is a gift from God. This is the example Christ gave the world.

It is easy to mouth many words; a little more difficult to understand the ramifications, the implicit meanings; and even more difficult to live accordingly. So, let us get right up front with the crux of the matter: if I should find this a meaningful, enjoyable experience, if I should grow and be able to lawfully live as a manifestation that is deserving of the gifts God so lovingly gives, I have not done anything. It will be the Father within who has made it all possible.

End of Entry

Over the course of the past two weeks, I have been very well prepared for this journey. I have had a number of opportunities to face many fears. As I meditated this afternoon, I thought about the fears I have looked at, though I realize it was all a matter of the preparation. I was also made aware this afternoon that the journey will not be as long as I anticipated it might be. The journey will begin Friday afternoon and it will end Sunday morning. That inner voice has made it very clear to me how much I have learned in my preparations. I have faced those bogiemen in the shower, those burglars in the night. I have recognized those things I was frightened of, was able to send them love, and they have disappeared. I will begin at a point identified as Black Rock Canyon, travel across Covington Flats into what is known as Ryans Camp, out across Jumbo Rocks, down through an area called Bell, and ultimately end my trip at the Oasis visitors center. This journey will begin from Joshua Lane, Highway 247, take me through a small part of the San Bernardino mountains, over through the Hexy mountains and out into the Twenty-Nine Palms area. A dear friend, Roy Bey, has agreed to drop me off at Joshua Tree.

End of Entry

I am fully conscious of the fact that this happens to be Easter weekend and that Christ was crucified on a Friday afternoon and resurrected on Sunday morning. But there are many things about this trip that challenge the empirical, intellectual side of me, give rise to doubts, and lead to conclusions that are not the kinds of conclusions I would like to admit. There is a side of me that says, What happened to your rational intellect? What happened to your understanding of psychology? Can you not see that there are many things functioning here that are giving rise to the absurd notion of the chase for a mystical experience, this overcoming fear which all men are born with? Can you not see what has been psychologically predisposed, that in one sense of the word you are operating as a schizophrenic, that you are denying your intellectual rational self? There is another side that says you really must be off the deep end, buddy, you are crazy! There is still another side of me that says that it is a thing that must be done. The nature of the journey, it appears now, does not take on the complexity or danger that I originally felt was associated with it. Maybe that is important. Maybe that outer other danger need not exist to the degree I had anticipated in order for me to more fully realize that the inner other real fear, the real monster that rests within. We might make a comparison to that of a photon with absolute potentiality and expression for matter and antimatter—positive or negative. I have the absolute potentiality, or you have the absolute potentiality, for expression in this physical universe as good or as evil. We must recognize that potentiality begins within. It seeks expression in the outer world through our activities and interaction with others, for if there were no others there would be no need for a world or for the individual manifestations or intelligence we view as man.

It is said that a drowning man sees his entire life in the flash of an instant. Somehow, I know that I will face every remnant, every remaining shred or scrap of fear that exist within me, and I will do so within this time frame, Friday night to Sunday morning. A dear friend of mine, a psychic in many senses, told me that the reason I was going to the desert was not really to face fear, but because I would be given a great gift there. The same person told me I would be there less than ten days unless I decide to exercise choice and stay much longer because I will be having so much fun. According to the instructions that are now clearly in front of me, I can see that I will be there for less than ten days. It will be most interesting to learn what this great gift is.

Today I saw a friend of a friend, a psychic who deals with and speaks of things from the other side, or the other side speaks through her. I was skeptical when we sat down, so I asked a number of questions. I was told that I was to make this journey, that I would be well rewarded for making it, and that I would find it very pleasurable. I was also told that I was to teach what Christ taught, that love is the only resolution to all of the problems the world faces, and that time was very urgent and limited in some ways. I have not accepted the idea of an Armageddon, simply because I can not conceive of the world ending, or of God ending the world when there is so many lessons to be learned. It seems to me that the world will cease to exist once there is no purpose for it—when there is only love. It was made clear to me today that it was not God who would end things but it was man, and that it was still not too late. I learned that if all consciousness would turn towards God and the principle of love, the teachings of Christ and the real meaning of those teachings would instantly alter the affairs of this world. I was also told that there was one other possibility—that a Soviet leader could turn the Soviets' attention towards Christ's behavior and Christ's teachings. God could also end it, and that too was a possibility; all possibilities rest within the choice of man. According to the choices that have been made, however, and as certain things have been set into motion, I knew that the time is short and my tasks are to be done with due haste.

Back to the synchronistic signs. In addition to receiving direction today regarding where I would be and how long I would be gone, I received intuitive guidance that I would find a certain shop. I did so while quite turned around in my bearings, and we stopped. It was there that I was to find a certain item, an amethyst quartz stone on a copper chain. I was very insistent with the clerk that she had such an item, but she claimed she did not. She searched thoroughly but there was no amethyst quartz and there was no copper chain. I stopped to visit with Roy a moment, and she spoke to the owner, a seventy-year-old man who has been in the business there for thirty years, and who is into holistic medicine and homeopathic care. This is a metaphysical shop that deals in stationery, jewelry, and herbs. After the clerk asked him about the amethyst quartz, he came over to talk to me. He pulled one out of his pocket and told me that while they carried the stones on a regular basis, the one in his pocket was sold, but if I wanted to check back with them they would have more. I told him I was from out-of-town and would not be in the area long, and asked if he could sell me that one. "No," he replied, "those in my pocket are not for sale." The one he had was for another customer, so I suggested he call the other customer, since I did not want to compromise any need the other customer had. I was equally sure the other customer would instruct him to let me have it. He phoned the customer, then came back and said, "Okay, I will sell you this one." I said "Fine; now I need a copper chain." He said, "I don't have copper chains." I insisted again, "I need it on a copper chain. I am sure you have a copper chain here somewhere." He said, "Wait a minute," and we walked around the counter and found a copper cross on a copper chain. So he used a gold chain for the copper cross and sold me the copper chain. I left with the amethyst quartz on a copper chain.

Anyone skilled in basic mathematics has to look at probabilities, and when we talk about consequences, there is a mathematical proposition that involves the nature of consequences. We can equate just how consequential or statistically meaningful some things are. Much in the way psychic abilities are tested, in the same manner I must look on these same synchronistic signs as being more of a consequence than a coincidence. There are many things we cannot explain, but the fact that we cannot explain them does not alter them. I am unable to find any logical reasoning to refute the nature of that which I observed, that which affected me, that which has acted upon me in the short period of preparing for this trip. This is not unique in my lifetime, for there have been many equally unique circumstances. I have paid particular attention to these, and as a result I have been able to examine them in a connected sort of way, not as an isolated "one here" and "one there," and there is clearly a picture that emerges. As children we connect numbered dots. When we first look at the page we see only black dots on a white background. Once we have connected them, we see a picture of a horse or some other animal. It is not usually necessary to connect all of the dots before we can see the picture. In the instance here, I have had many dots, and enough of those dots have been connected for me to state unequivocally that this is much more than coincidence. The picture I see is clearly the picture that I anticipated seeing.

Tomorrow I will continue this log. I will attempt to do so with times, in the hope that perhaps it will make a little more sense. To conclude this entry, I believe that love is truly a matter of letting go of fear, and as Mr. Nagal, the spirit that came through Connie today, stated, that Heaven is here.

Friday, April 5, 1985

This morning I awoke at 4:30 A.M. I am a little apprehensive. The complexity of this trip has changed so many times.

Journey Begins

It is noon, and I am in Joshua Tree National Monument, about forty-five minutes from where Roy dropped me. I have already seen a lot of wildlife— rabbits, birds, lizards—but you are alone out here. There is a vast immensity of desert; it's peaceful! I guess this is what I came for—just me. I think that is what this trip has all come down to—not a test of survival, not a challenge of the old things, not some old Death Valley days I survived— it is to be alone with me. That is probably where the fear comes from, not from anywhere else. Just me. Terribly tragic when you think about a grown man who reaches forty years of age and has climbed just about every mountain he has ever wanted to climb, done just about anything he has ever wanted to do, and who his friends consider to be courageous, but who is really afraid of being with just himself. I suppose in facing that fear I will be able to let go of many other categorical fears, although sitting here now is not terrifying at all. Still, it is broad daylight and I know that there is a campground within forty-five minutes from here. It has outside toilets and other people. That might have something to do with it. Time will tell. Roy and I talked earlier about how all this doesn't have anything to do with conquering anything. It is a matter of having to face and embrace and love some things about myself, maybe laugh at myself and get truly in touch with myself. So I will use this opportunity to remember that Christ died this afternoon and raised himself on Sunday. Despite all his friends he was alone; he was in touch with himself, in harmony with God and the Universe.

On the way to this point there were two Joshua trees, the tops of which were some twenty feet in the air and growing eight to ten feet apart. They stood side by side like an archway. I made a step to the left and passed through the archway, a symbolic recognition of the journey I am about to take.

Okay, after a ten-minute break, I am going to continue on. I am not sure where I will be going, but will just trust my intuition. As I walk and think of things from time to time, I will just turn the recorder on and enter those things as they come. I remember last night thinking that there would be no test that I could not pass. I think about that as I wander through the sage-brush. I see various forms of cacti and I think about the rattlesnakes. Those "white man rattlesnakes." The desert floor is marvelous. It does not change in appearance other than density. The sandy base of it looks like clean, washed gravel in an aquarium, yet at the same time it is very hard in some places, like walking on a sidewalk, and soft in others; it just sort of spins out from underneath your feet like walking in a sandpile. Very illusionary. I wish you could hear the birds. I have stopped where there is an abundance of wildlife. There has to be fifty to sixty birds. If only I knew a little more about birds! Perhaps I could tell you they're smaller than sparrows, fly much like dove, and sound beautiful. I would defy someone to tell me these birds are not a band of angels right here on earth. Walking through the desert is kind of like walking through life. If you are in a hurry to get from point A to point B, you miss much of the beauty of the desert in bloom, of things you have no names for. It just overwhelms me that the animals and wildlife seem to accept me as a part of the desert. They neither hide nor flee. How diverse the earth is from her homo sapien children. Deserts are not only barren, there is so much beauty it is just marvelous.

Flowers that look like miniature sunflowers, not much larger than blades of grass, cover the sand. Oh, I wish I had read a little about the desert before coming here, and could then describe to you what I have seen. I could give each thing a name and with its name you could look it up in a book. There in living color you could witness some of its beauty, and yet not behold it at all. How much our lives and that which we sense and feel and smell in every way are like the descriptions of flowers in the desert.

I have found a magic place due south of where Roy dropped me. I have been wandering around in it for a while. It is completely surrounded by boulders, the likes of which you would have to see to believe. The unique thing is that the small stones are on the bottom and the large stones are on the top, looking like huge dinosaur eggs laid thousands of years ago. This is the place in which I have to face myself. This is an Oasis. There is no visible water and yet there is much greenery, much wildlife, and it is completely surrounded by boulders that must be thirty feet high. I can only guess at the thousands and thousands of pounds they must weigh. There is one opening on the north end and one on the south end, otherwise it is a fort of thousand-pound (or probably more) rocks. Solitary rocks have been dumped on each other like a child would stack stones in the street. Now, that is something a geologist can tell me about one day.

This little hideaway is approximately sixty feet across from east to west. After looking it over good, I suppose I will wait at the west end until I am shaded from the sun, and I can just move back and forth in this little valley, and never have to leave. I do not want to mislead you though; this valley overlooks almost everything except the mountain range, which is perhaps another hour walk. It is a beautiful place. I am very glad I was not forced into this, where I might regret or resent it. It is one thing to be marooned alone, or to be abandoned, or to be in hiding and afraid of someone else, but it is an altogether different thing to choose to be all alone for a protracted period of time without support systems, just to genuinely get in touch with yourself. You know, it is funny, but all week long I have not shaved. This morning I got up and shaved and there is not a soul in this desert that cares or will even notice. Strange things.

A dear friend of mine gave me some words to bring here and I mulled them over in my mind as I was getting in the habit of timing and dating the entries on the recorder so that when they are converted to paper they have some semblance of order. The words had to do with a man who had to face temptations. He faced them during one evening. All he had to do was to see through the illusions of each temptation and see reality. These words had to do with allowing the Father within to do his battle. The Father within would be the warrior for him. He was to have courage and understand that he was in battle, but not to fight, not to resist, not to run; to trust to the Father was his task. Those words have become for me a pounding percussion right this minute.

I am looking west. I can see for miles, since everything goes downhill. It is immense; it is beautiful. Legend has it that this area, Joshua Tree National Monument, was holy and sacred to the Indians. They journeyed here at least once every year. Their shaman and medicine men practiced their secrets and saw many visions. It is interesting that I would choose to come here. I am certain that where I have chosen to stay is certainly a place that would have caught the attention, captured the imagination, of the wisest Indian shaman. How I wish I had brought a camera! I would love to have everyone see what I have seen, but of course it would not have been the same as seeing it for one's self.

I saw my first rattlesnake and he is a big one. Just lying back in the shade in the cracks where I thought I would snuggle down. Since he and I are not apt to become the best of friends (despite the fact I do not intend for us to become enemies), I think I will defer to his power and find myself another place for some shade and take a little nap. I am looking at a cactus which you would not believe. It looks like a small flocked Christmas tree, and it sparkles all over. Incredible! Pineapple cactus it must be. It looks like the pineapple fruit. Beautiful purple flowers are coming into bloom, opening at the end, with canopy-like pods. I do not know what these things are called, but it is ever so beautiful here. This must have all been under water at one time. I have been looking at a beautiful piece of natural sculpture, and as I get close to it I see that there are thousands of tiny little rocks such as you would find on a seashore. They are embedded and stuck one upon another so that it is not one big rock, but it is hundreds of tiny little rocks. Man could not have done anything this magnificent.

I am going to continue to venture around in my little habitat for a while. I am certain that where I am was at one time a shoreline. As I look at the rocks now, a light, new pattern of geometry emerges. The desert floor, with its softness and its hardness, now has some meaning to me. Still, I regret not studying about the desert before making this journey. I felt it was important that I come here like a child, all senses open, so that everything that I beheld would be new, intriguing, and beautiful. Perhaps, as in the letters from Eve translated by Mark Twain, I could create a formula such as H_2O plus a property indigenous to the atmosphere. There is such beauty, and yet I have not the words (or without studying, I do not have names), and without the names there seems to be an inability to communicate what I am talking about. I quickly run out of words or the words become redundant. Words do not communicate what I sense or see. If I attempt to describe to you this strange bush in front of me or this little white flower on the end of a branch, I do not know where to begin, other than to say I am looking at a strange bush. Understand that even if I were capable of giving it to you precisely, it would not be the same as seeing it. Words are only an approximation, and I am sure that if you saw the same thing, you would likely see it differently. What I find strangely marvelous, exciting, and beautiful, you may find mundane, boring, and dry. Nevertheless, with nearly as much naivite (at least about the desert), as Adam and Eve had in discovering all about the marvelous earth after partaking of that fruit of the tree, I have the opportunity to discover all about everything that surrounds me and that occupies my thoughts and so much of myself. It is hard to think of myself when I am surrounded by so much history, so much grandeur, so much immenseness. It is somehow difficult to take on the permanence, the nobility of civilized man. Perhaps it is the animals that truly are at peace. Man can label it and call it peace, but does not comprehend peace at all.

I choose carefully where to sit down and stretch out my legs and take advantage of the shade, for I do not want to disturb the plants. I would like to camp in a way that when I leave, someone else coming into this place like I did could say that no human had been here for a very long time. Yet as I stretch out, I lengthened my toes and my heels slipped on the ground and tore some young blades of grass out of the earth. Despite our best attempts at avoiding such things, I wonder just how much life is lost in such unthinking ways or without notice.

These giant rock formations are literally riddled with caves, passages, and tunnels. The only sign of human life is an occasional aircraft, and I guess from the speeds they are out of Nellis Air Force Base. I can hear screeching from some very large, or what sounds like very large, birds nearby, but I cannot see them. I guess I will just kick back and wait until dusk. In a sense I must admit being somewhat disappointed. I have looked forward to this journey with apprehension and excitement for the last couple of weeks, but now that I am here, it is so peaceful and quiet. So little going on. I don't have anything to do. I guess I brought with me the mental garbage from our civilized society, and I probably do not even know how to do nothing. I suppose most people know little about how to do absolutely nothing. I would be remiss if I did not admit that somehow my expectations are not as keen as they were. I do not feel there is going to be any spectacular experience at all. Perhaps what I am experiencing now is my total realization. I guess I'll just sort of mellow down and see if I can learn to do absolutely nothing.

I am reminded that this is Good Friday, 1985, that years ago Christ of Nazareth died on a cross sometime in the late afternoon, probably about now. Those thoughts and thoughts of all history that has existed in this particular place seem to occupy my mind and provide the little activity of my intellect. As I think about it, I become less and less aware of anything in the environment. It is as if I had become a seed, just floating along in the air without any real destination. I don't suppose it really matters much where I end up. Sooner or later I will sprout or I won't, but for a while I felt like a seed floating along with absolutely no care in the world.

Franklin Roosevelt said that the only thing to fear is fear itself. Fear seems to be the unknown level of expectation, an apprehension of something that we seldom really see. How strange it is that we choose to live in the future or the past, when the present is all we ever have. I anticipated being afraid that I would be in some immense, unfamiliar country alone, with no support systems, cut off, and that I would be frightened. Instead, it is so very peaceful, so pleasurable. This is an easy fear to look at, to embrace, and to love;

but then wait until dark. Only men and birds seem to be around in the light of day. The rest of the desert comes alive in the evening, when the snakes come out, along with the bobcats and coyotes and other predators. That is when man seems to be vulnerable. After all, we rely so much on sight. I have been educated to understand that man's first weapon was fire. Oh, he had stones perhaps and clubs, but his first line of defense, safety, and security, was fire. Hovering in a cave with a fire burning, there really was no night. I have no fire, so I will face the sightless nature of a strange place tonight.

If my theory is right, where there is no separateness, there is no threat. If there is no threat, there is no fear. We take for granted that wild animals become vicious when terrified and cornered, and yet man operates on an equally vicious scale, but more often in defense of things like his ego. He is, of course, frightened. The difference is so immense. I heard the chatter of those large birds again. I turned, saw an outline, and thought it was an eagle. I could have sworn it was an eagle. I watched its silhouette as it seemed to move, to land upon a Joshua tree. Just a blossom at the end of the tree. I wonder if our fears are rather like our illusions. We see what we expect or would like to see.

Trust ourselves, as the Master says, and trust no one else, but perhaps ourselves are the greatest deluders of all. It takes a long time for the sun to go down in the desert. Shadows seem to get longer and longer and the birds get quieter. I have managed to conjure up monster after monster, some from this world and some from other worlds. As night approaches, I would be less than candid to say I had not given a thought to leaving this place. I suppose we feed our fears by trying to run away from them, just as we support our fears by denying them, and acting out our heroism in the light of day before others to prove our personal worth. Out here there is not a lot of personal worth in the great grand scheme of the rocks and Joshua trees, or the cacti that is several hundred years old, or the sand aged beyond the comprehension of time. Out here, if you have a fear, you can really give it power because there is not anyone or anything to turn your thoughts from it. It is easy to concentrate on anything that is fearful as it is to dwell on some particularly joyful and pleasurable thought. If I concede that bogiemen go bump in the night, I am going to have many of them. I realize that for me there is only one fear left, fear in the deep, dark sense of the word, and that fear is a fear of myself. If some fool ever tells you to take a trip out into the desert, walk as far as you can, make sure you're out of sight, sound, and range of any other human being, merge yourself in with the rocks and critters, and not to bring a flashlight, candle, or match, but take only the bare necessities; if someone ever tells you to do that, you are plumb crazy to do it unless it is an inner self that gives the instructions. Then I suppose you must do what you must do.

When I think of it now, I am not afraid of surviving in any sense of that word. That is a contest; that is what I have done all my life. It must be that element of surprise, of the unknown, of not being prepared. I suppose that fear is rooted in always having to be in control.

How can we be afraid of something we know, if it does not injure us? This is a marvelous desert and a marvelous experience. I have concluded that I can handle this world, and the Father within can handle all else. I know I will awaken in the morning and I will feel silly about all this, much ado about nothing.

The mountain west of me has a tower on it, apparently an air traffic tower. I can see the red lights flashing below a beacon. The desert is growing very quiet. The temperature has dropped. I feel very much at peace. Contrary to what you see in the city, the heavens are full of stars. I remember when I was a child and slept outside. There were stars after stars after stars— countless stars. Nowadays in the larger cities where our children grow up, they truly think they can count all the stars there are on two hands. There is a very large hawk perched about two hundred feet away from me. I trust the hawk is going to watch for the kangaroo rats and other creatures that might interfere with a good night's sleep. I sort of feel like he is sitting there watching me.

It is 3:00 A.M. and the desert is beautiful. Perhaps a lesson I was to learn was not just to let go of my own personal fears, but to realize one of the laws of this universe—interdependence. The system of the desert depends upon each part, not altogether different from the system in the human environment. The real meaning, I suppose, of the law of interdependence is not just that we depend upon one another, or *need* to depend upon one another, but that we must appreciate each other. Somehow, I think I am going to find myself a little more appreciative when in the company of another human being. Perhaps I can have a conversation, even with a human being that annoys me, and remember that an annoying one is better than no one.

I just saw a shooting star. It has been a long time since I have seen one. There are many rites of passage, and I have one other behind me: at least one of the lessons tonight here is that God created all. One is not saved without the other, anymore than the wildlife of the desert—the plants and the animals—exist without each other.

In my dreams, or with my eyes closed, I have seen many forms this evening —some much more terrifying than others. I have given them love, embraced them, healed them with the universal white light of life, recognized them, and felt no separateness. Each time the terror has left there has been a vision of Christ. In my dreams? Perhaps it is something I ate, something in the night air, something that I expected, something psychologically predisposed. Whatever it is, from whatever source or form— reality or in the eye of the mind only—it has released me from all fear.

Many consciousness's linger with me now, as guides and masters. I will trust in them.

Morning of the second day.

It is the morning of the second day and it is an exquisitely beautiful morning. I have received many marvelous gifts and I shall take them with me.

This morning I was able to truly quiet my mind, shut external stimuli out, and sense that other internal voice. It was marvelous and I was told many things. It is true—be still and know. I have much work ahead of me when I return. There are many things which must be said and which must be done. I have such a glorious opportunity to testify to the glory of God, and that which God has given all! It is my observation that the single largest inhibiting factor to these internal voices is that when we hear them we begin a dialogue, a dialogue between two selves. We sort of talk back and forth to ourselves about what it was we heard. We apply a rational empirical criteria and then we operate from an absolute situation of doubt.

It is a marvelous time to be in the desert. I am sure that when my friends awoke this morning they said thank you as I did. It is said that when God created the earth and created life forms, he endowed each with particular qualities; some were to be cowardly, some were to be timid, some were to be brave. Then he created man, and to man he gave all the qualities of all his creations—the beast, the fowl, the insect, the reptile—and then he gave to man the ability to choose which he would manifest in his lifetime.

The birds play with the birds, the lizards play with the lizards and two black beetles trek the same trail. They all have predators, but do not prey upon each other. All this harshness and there is still beauty. If I refuse to look at the beautiful rather than that which I call harsh (or less), I seemingly change the perception. I can affect the perception of others, for someone who might hear these words that has not thought of this place and of all its splendor. And yet, I can tell you that the ground is burned in many places; there is death, decay, waste, hardship. The heat is relentless and the marks it has left on nature awesome. The land is desolate as far as one can see. Even the mountains are treeless. Only the Joshua trees break the monotonous desolation.

Just how powerful are our perceptions? Joshua trees are in bloom, but their bark is rough and the trees look rather homely. If I tell you how beautiful the desert is in the spring and I choose only to look upon and describe the new life, the blossoms in full bloom, you will see a marvelous place; but if I tell you about the stump of an old Joshua tree that I am now looking at— burned black, worn haggard, decayed, infested with tiny insect life chewing away at it—what you see is what I perceive and describe. It is a shame that all of us cannot behold beauty, communicate beauty, see only beauty, realize the great gifts that are ours by inheritance, and give of those gifts freely. There is no limitation to the abundance with which nature overwhelms us. This is a strange world indeed.

I found a rock formation that is like a huge outdoor swimming pool. I can see where the water has receded, perhaps thousands of years ago. It is incredible to think that this desert at one time was a lakeshore or under water. I can only guess at all the secrets that could be told in this land.

The way some of these rocks jet up into the air, and the way they are cut around the bottom as if water had washed on them for thousands of years, intrigues me. I wonder what the arches of Achilles that Socrates spoke about when describing the lost continent of Atlantis would look like. I suspect somewhat like this. It's fun to fantasize about sailing between these rocks.

It is unfortunate that all men do not get to know their Maker in this life and some men cannot seem to get in touch with their ultimate reality.

Where I have camped there are squirrels and finches that I have been feeding. There is one little squirrel that has no fear at all. As long as I don't move, it will come within inches of me, picking up little yogurt-coated almonds and sunflower seeds. I have finches all around me. It is like a little oasis, though I am not aware of the presence of water here.

I intuitively know I have no reason to stay longer. I have learned that which I came to learn; but it is so pleasant I will stay at least another night. This evening I will sort of kick back and enjoy all that God has to offer in this great creation of his, and give thanks for my ability to do so.

It is amazing how things have changed in the short time I have been here. I refuse to pull a lump of grass out of the ground. I move my bed instead. I was able to sit down on a rock with a lizard today, and the lizard wasn't one bit afraid of me. Nature seems to have a sense that seems to know whether you are there to destroy or there to just kind of prowl, to become a part of the wind and the grass and the creatures. Nature says it all in the way that she treats man. Moreover, man also makes a statement in the way he treats nature.

I lay down on the desert floor today, drank in the sun, felt it beat down on me—for a moment just drifted away and became a pebble of sand, shining, flittering, absorbing the light from high in the heavens above. A most delightful experience. Simple beauty is simply truth!

Man has a way of wanting to complicate life; he yearns to dissect the frog in the perverable sense, to understand every tendon, every ligament, but he is never able to put it back together. We have applied electric shock and watched the legs jerk, but much of it we had never seen in its totality as a frog. My good friend Christian says man has a propensity for desiring to take things apart instead of evaluating them. Well, I evaluated the sand today as the sun beat down on it. I joined it for a while. Like the sand, I went unburned.

As I sit in the shade awaiting nightfall, it occurs to me that life in the desert is a way of nonresistance. Life would perish here through resistance. To survive, the living must embrace itself as natural, as beautiful, and do so gratefully. Man is the only creature that pretends to be what he is not.

I have had all day to relfect. I have discovered that whenever I become angry with someone, it is because of a fear or insecurity in myself. When I made imaptient demands on other people, for the most part it was an insecurity in myself. When I saw and spoke with someone who annoyed or irritated me, I saw something of myself I did not like in that someone. I have not yet been able to think of one thing in the world that upsets me or makes me angry that is not somehow a lesson teaching me about a weakness of my own. I have not yet been able to think of one thing in the world that is served by anger, hostility, or aggression. I think I have learned many things. Will I be able to live them? Christ taught us to love our brother. I see the birds, and the finches fly with the finches; I watch the lizards and they have no separateness between themselves; it amazes me that human beings separate themselves so much from other human beings.

Roy told me the other evening of two women he saw sitting in a lounge in a Las Vegas casino. These two women were approximately the same age—and sat two stools apart for most of the evening. Both of them seemed sad, but the saddest part was that they were so close and had so much opportunity, yet neither spoke to the other. It is as if we are afraid to let someone in on who we are. We are afraid to open our arms and love another as we do our brother. If we could look at every man, woman, and child that walked the earth as the image of Christ; if we could see the Christ in them instead of the opposite, what one of us would not race to embrace them? Can we not see that every human being on this earth is our brother? That there is a Christ consciousness in them, and as the Great Master said, whatever we do unto the least of our brethren we do unto him.

It occurs to me that despite our language, man still communicates in thought. I am sure that if I thought by grabbing that lizard, as I might have done as a child, it would have run instead of remaining on the rock with me. There must have been a time before language when man's thoughts were as open as his deeds. But don't be so sure that his thoughts are not becoming his deeds in this day and age. Maybe as a race we lack the sensitivity necessary to perceive the cause and effect—the thought and the deed. One of the marvelous gifts given me is the ability to listen to inner voices. I have learned to use thought as a form of communication to all around me. I have been guided in that way and I have avoided possible calamities in that way, but what's more, the balance, peace, and harmony that I have never known I cannot include here. A marvelous future awaits us.

Just a little postscript here for the purpose of levity. I trust that as I wait for nightfall, I won't have to convince those damn mosquitoes to leave me alone.

They say to bring your own wood to the park because there is no firewood to burn. Of course there isn't anything like maple, oak or poplar firewood, but there is plenty of deadfall to burn. Cactus burns well, as a matter of fact. I am enjoying a small fire right now, though it is not as cool tonight as it was last night. Perhaps the fire is the difference. Boy Scout lore often comes in handy.

I saw mountain climbers earlier. The man in front had already ascended, and there were two women at the bottom, each coaxing the other on. From time to time, the man complained about what he was doing up there. The man would snap harsh words at the women down below. Maybe it is just my new perspective, but it was so obvious that when he snapped he was attempting to conceal his fears. His aggression and hostility was only a method of compensating for his fears. I saw so much of myself in that young man.

Cactus coals burn differently than anything I have ever seen. They burn almost like a spiritual fire. They flash louder, retreat and flash loudly in the flame once again. Almost as if there is some kind of oxygen or chemical inside the root of this particular cactus. Chemical or oxygen? It is as if someone threw gunpowder on the fire from time to time. I burned a small rotten trunk of a Joshua tree. Now that the coals have burned down, I can see that the trunk is the sole heat producer now. it is still burning. Everything else is just simmering out. Quite a combination for a fire—a cactus root that looks like a pineapple, and a Joshua tree.

I rest my body and give thanks. Thank you, thank you, thank you.

Note:

On the morning of the third day I ceased all entries on the recorder. I arose *knowing* at levels I had never even contemplated existing. *Knowing* is something that each of us must do for ourselves.

On Expectation

Expectation is like nuclear power. Properly harnessed it yields delightful rewards. Negatively focused it delightfully delivers the expectation.

The absence of expectation is natural. In acceptance expectation dissolves. Expectation is conditional.

In Disneyland, with expectation as the instrument to realization, turn the instrument into coins that operate only the *fun* rides. In the eternal now realized, the coins and the rides are only an illusion.

Consider . . . Ultimate Reality

A Channeled Transmission

All that is, IS energy. Consciousness IS. Our being conscious of being conscious is not Consciousness. Our individualized consciousness is in evolution. Consciousness IS. Consciousness is out of time and space, while being conscious individually creates the illusion of time, space and separateness.

Thought is "reality-one." In a schema of thought reality there exists "reality one" by some exponential value that becomes Consciousness. The inevitable, ineffable ONENESS IS realized in complete immersion with the IS Consciousness.

Thinking is destiny. Every atom in the physical world, every thought form in the unmanifested sphere is a product of thought activity. Thinking is a thought activity. Unconscious and subconscious processes are also thought activities. Selecting and owning all of our thought activity is being conscious of creating our reality. Choosing realities is the mission of life— each life. The individual is a facet in the One Mind—the IS Consciousness.

You are the world, a world unto your self and a co-creator to individualized other worlds.

Reality is relative. Just as no two people can possibly observe exactly the same incident, no two people can share the same simultaneous physical reality.

Illusion rests in consensus. To agree to accept a reality is to create/co-create *a* reality based on this expectation. Illusion authors purpose. Purpose claims absolutes. Thus, constructs such as karma and dharma are born. Right and wrong, sin and piety, good and evil become the score measurement for purpose. Purpose is illusion.

Truth IS. Consciousness is Truth. Transcendence is escaping illusion. Giving oneself up to and for others is rising beyond the limitations of self-boundaries. Direction (purpose) is in Consciousness. The IS Consciousness transcends the being conscious of being conscious.

Thought is often confined by trained expectation. Genius is thought outside confinement. Inspiration is thought without processing. In an instant a flash of "knowing" occurs, and as a result of thought there exists a simultaneous realization of the occurrence. Thought then translates the occurrence usually for purposes of communication.

Thinking in the real sense convolutes the models. One gets out of the process of thinking to get into the dimension of thought. A simple example of this "out of" model can be expressed in the classical nine-dot matrix problem:

$$\begin{matrix} \bullet & \bullet & \bullet \\ \bullet & \bullet & \bullet \\ \bullet & \bullet & \bullet \end{matrix}$$

(Connect all of the dots with four straight lines without lifting your writing instrument from the page.)

Every single aspect of the physical, including the biological you, is fundamentally a wave form manifested in large according to expectation. The collective expectation is the collective unconscious of Jung. The collective unconscious is not the IS Consciousness; rather it is an aspect of the thinking patterns and processes of mind individualized—a reservoir of electromagnetic resonance existing at different harmonic levels. There is a synergistic effect to thinking patterns. This is why the "form" transcends the limitations of the "particular."

Ultimately each and all of all is light; wave form manifest from the light (electromagnetic continuum) into the physical. This is what is meant by maya, or illusion. The proposition is not to deny the physical, opting for "other-worldly" over "this-worldly," but to see the illusion. Seeing the illusion (physically) for what the illusion is can free one from the limited expectation inherent in this implied paradox.

All thought is wave form. Only wave form exists. Thus, thinking is destiny! The Law is thought. The Law operates from Unconditional Love. Nothing exists except that it is a gift. The FIRST CAUSE gifted individual expression to unformed thought. Thought took up thinking and thus the individual evolution of *aspects* of "being in consciousness" began.

If the individualized manifestation is less than unconditional love, Oneness with all, then the particular remains but a shadow of the form—thinking exists until it becomes thought in the IS Consciousness. By convoluting models, paradoxes are found.

The secret of mastery is moving Thinking from the "take" to the "give" expectation mode. Unconditional giving is Divine. Destiny presupposes future—future is illusion. Thinking becomes thought when emulating the Divine.

The evolution of "being conscious" of "being conscious" becomes the IS Consciousness when the I becomes One. Unconditional Love is giving not from the I perspective but from the I. This is indeed when the "Father and I become one."

The only philosophy in life that endures beyond the physical is the three "R's." All reality is built upon relationships. Even the collective unconscious, or collective expectation, that holds the wave form in a continuum of manifestation and thus produces the physical world, is a relational interaction. Our reality therefore is first, last and always only relative to our relationships. The philosophy is simple: Relative Relationship Reality is all there is. Know this and you know all.

P.S. The solution to the nine-dot matrix:

Problem   Solution

```
 •   •   •
 •   •   •
 •   •   •
```

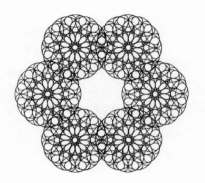